Mindful Moments

Volume 1
The Inner Work That Will Rock Your Outer World!™

A. Drayton Boylston

INTERNATIONAL
MINDFULNESS
FEDERATION™

ISBN-13: 978-0-9749314-3-2

Published by International Mindfulness Federation Press
www.IMFSite.com

Edited & Prepared for Publication by Jennifer-Crystal Johnson
www.JenniferCrystalJohnson.com

Written by A. Drayton Boylston
www.ExecutiveCoachingUniversity.com

Although the author and publisher have made every effort to ensure that the information in this book was correct at press time, the author and publisher do not assume and hereby disclaim any liability to any party for any loss, damage, or disruption caused by errors or omissions, whether such errors or omissions result from negligence, accident, or any other cause.

This book is not intended as a substitute for the medical advice of physicians. The reader should regularly consult a physician in matters relating to his/her health and particularly with respect to any symptoms that may require diagnosis or medical attention.

"Meditation is not a way of making your mind quiet. It's a way of entering into the quiet that's already there—buried under the 60,000 thoughts the average person has every day."

Deepak Chopra

Dedication

To all the courageous souls who are seeking more… and are willing to take the time to dive deeper.

Hooray, that's you!

Also by A. Drayton Boylston

A Whisper From Your Soul™
More Whispers From Your Soul™
Coming UnScrooged! A Contemporary Classic of
Corporate Rescue and Redemption
The Mindful Leader Workshop™
The Certified Mindful Leader™
The Mindful Mentor Program™
The Mindful Leader Blog™
The Active Exec Program™
The Life Purpose Workbook™
The Coaching Crucible™
The Sage and Scholars Guide to Coaching
Executives™
Coaching in the Workplace™

Rescued Executive Series:
Coach as Lifeguard™
Executive CPR™
Coach as EMT™
Rescued Executive Chronicles™
Whispers From Your Soul Blog™

To sign up for more mindfulness resources,
please visit:
http://www.executivecoachinguniversity.com/m
indfulness-movement

Table of Contents

Foreword

What is a Mindful Moment and why should I take time for them?

You're busy, right?

Feeling a bit stressed?

Wondering if there is more to life?

I sure was… until I made the shift to working on being more mindful.

You see, I'm a "recovering" CEO who almost killed himself working. Literally.

I hope that what I've learned along my journey around the power of mindfulness helps you on yours.

That's it.

Time to get started….

"Not being able to stop thinking is an affliction, but we don't realize this because almost everyone is suffering from it."

Eckhart Tolle

How to Use This Journal

We'll keep this simple and straightforward. Otherwise, experience tells me that you won't use this.

Given that the average book buyer only reads 17 pages of any book they buy, I want this experience to stick... throughout the entire year. 17 pages is only a delicious appetizer.

We made the journal a smaller size and with six months' worth of pages in order to keep it small, so you can carry it around if you choose to. We hope this works well for you.

About the Daily Prompts

I am grateful for...

More than likely you will start out with the obvious things like family, health, etc. Your real growth comes when you choose to go deeper. You start to find small things to be grateful for that you may never have even noticed previously. A flower, the giggle of a baby... your very next breath. When you are in a state of gratitude, you are truly being mindful. And… one of the cool things about this is that the more you express gratitude for what you have, the more you seem to get what you are grateful for. Amazing, huh?!

My Mindful Moments today…

These are the times when you really felt like you were fully present. Times you felt "in the flow." Moments when you felt like nothing else mattered except for what you were doing *right now*. Those blissful moments when the past didn't matter, the future wasn't a concern… that that very moment was all there was. You see, that is where the truth lies… for there is only the present moment. Everything else is an illusion of our own creation.

Thought to ponder as I sleep…

This is a very powerful tool. Given that we spend almost a third of our lives sleeping, wouldn't it make sense to put it to good use? Most folks never even think about anything but closing their eyes and trying to forget all their worries of the day. Science now tells us that our brains are hard at work even when we sleep. This prompt will put yours to work on things that you need to get some answers to. All you have to do is pick a word or a sentence that you would like to ponder as you sleep. Say that word or sentence silently to yourself as you move into slumber. Your brain will take that thought and work on it as you sleep. You don't have to do anything else... other than be curious and receptive to new thoughts about this subject that may arise the next day. Since your brain was working on this all through the night, some amazing and different insights may pop into your awareness.

Step 1
Take three deeeeep breaths for me.

1...
2...
3...

Excellent! You're off to a brilliant start.
Now, do that each night before you pick up your journal.

Step 2
Open your Mindful Moments Journal to any page that feels right. By design, there are no

dates on the pages. Pick whatever page speaks to you.

Step 3

Do what feels right. You may read the quote for the day. Writing down some things you are grateful for may speak to you. Recalling your Mindful Moments during the day may inspire you. Creating a positive thought to experience as you sleep may catch your attention.

You may want to write.
You may not.
Go inside.
Ask yourself what feels right.

Cast no judgment on your actions or decisions.

Observe your choices. Hover above them.

Truly *feel* what you *feel* as you open each page.

Breathe....
The beauty is in each breath as you let yourself experience this moment.

The act of focusing on this moment is key.

Choose to live your life *now*.

Not in the regrets of yesterday...
or the worries of tomorrow.

Now.

You see,
in reality...
that is all we really have.

Now.

Let's Get Started!

As you get going, remember that it all comes down to this:

"Be happy in the moment; that's enough. Each moment is all we need, nothing more."

Mother Teresa

The greatest trip you will ever take is within yourself. Enjoy this beautiful journey of your own creation.

Wishing you peace, joy, and love as you write, go quiet, and grow.

With love!

Drayton and everyone at the International Mindfulness Federation

And…

Remember to breathe.

1…
2…
3…

I knew you were going to pick this up quickly!

Mindful Moments

"You must live in the present, launch yourself on every wave, find your eternity in each moment. Fools stand on their island of opportunities and look toward another land. There is no other land; there is no other life but this."

Henry David Thoreau

I am grateful for...

_____

_____

_____

_____

My Mindful Moments today...

_____

_____

_____

_____

Thought to ponder as I sleep...

_____

_____

_____

_____

"All of the man's difficulties are caused by his inability to sit, quietly, in a room by himself."

Blaise Pascal

I am grateful for...

_____

_____

_____

_____

My Mindful Moments today…

_____

_____

_____

_____

Thought to ponder as I sleep...

_____

_____

_____

_____

"If you are doing mindfulness meditation, you are doing it with your ability to attend to the moment."

Daniel Goleman

I am grateful for...

_____

_____

_____

_____

My Mindful Moments today…

_____

_____

_____

Thought to ponder as I sleep...

_____

_____

_____

_____

"Mindfulness isn't difficult; we just need to remember to do it."

Sharon Salzberg

I am grateful for...

My Mindful Moments today…

Thought to ponder as I sleep...

"If you want to conquer the anxiety of life, live in the moment, live in the breath."

Amit Ray

I am grateful for...

My Mindful Moments today...

Thought to ponder as I sleep...

"One is a great deal less anxious if one feels perfectly free to be anxious, and the same may be said of guilt."

Alan W. Watts

I am grateful for...

_____

_____

_____

_____

My Mindful Moments today...

_____

_____

_____

_____

Thought to ponder as I sleep...

_____

_____

_____

_____

"To pay attention, this is our endless and proper work."

Mary Oliver

I am grateful for...

_____

_____

_____

_____

My Mindful Moments today…

_____

_____

_____

_____

Thought to ponder as I sleep...

_____

_____

_____

_____

"If someone comes along and shoots an arrow into your heart, it's fruitless to stand there and yell at the person. It would be much better to turn your attention to the fact that there's an arrow in your heart...."

Pema Chödrön

I am grateful for...

_____

_____

_____

_____

My Mindful Moments today...

_____

_____

_____

_____

Thought to ponder as I sleep...

_____

_____

_____

_____

"Happiness, not in another place but this place... not for another hour, but this hour."

Walt Whitman

I am grateful for...

My Mindful Moments today…

Thought to ponder as I sleep...

"Empty your mind, be formless, shapeless—like water. Now you put water into a cup, it becomes the cup; you put water into a bottle, it becomes the bottle; you put it in a teapot, it becomes the teapot. Now water can flow or it can crash. Be water, my friend."

Bruce Lee

I am grateful for...

My Mindful Moments today...

Thought to ponder as I sleep...

"Perfection of character is this: to live each day as if it were your last, without frenzy, without apathy, without pretense."

Marcus Aurelius

I am grateful for...

_____

_____

_____

_____

My Mindful Moments today...

_____

_____

_____

_____

Thought to ponder as I sleep...

_____

_____

_____

_____

"If the doors of perception were cleansed, everything would appear to man as it is: infinite."
William Blake

I am grateful for...

_____

_____

_____

_____

My Mindful Moments today...

_____

_____

_____

_____

Thought to ponder as I sleep...

_____

_____

_____

_____

"Most of us take for granted that time flies, meaning that it passes too quickly. But in the mindful state, time doesn't really pass at all. There is only a single instant of time that keeps renewing itself over and over with infinite variety."

Deepak Chopra

I am grateful for...

My Mindful Moments today...

Thought to ponder as I sleep...

"Our own worst enemy cannot harm us as much as our unwise thoughts. No one can help us as much as our own compassionate thoughts."

Buddha

I am grateful for...

_____

_____

_____

_____

My Mindful Moments today...

_____

_____

_____

_____

Thought to ponder as I sleep...

_____

_____

_____

_____

"Mindfulness helps us freeze the frame so that we can become aware of our sensations and experiences as they are, without the distorting coloration of socially conditioned responses or habitual reactions."

Henepola Gunaratana

I am grateful for...

_____

_____

_____

_____

My Mindful Moments today...

_____

_____

_____

_____

Thought to ponder as I sleep...

_____

_____

_____

_____

"One does not become enlightened by imagining figures of light, but by making the darkness conscious. The latter procedure, however, is disagreeable and therefore not popular."

C.G. Jung

I am grateful for...

_____

_____

_____

_____

My Mindful Moments today…

_____

_____

_____

_____

Thought to ponder as I sleep...

_____

_____

_____

_____

"Don't believe everything you think. Thoughts are just that—thoughts."

Allan Lokos

I am grateful for...

_____

_____

_____

_____

My Mindful Moments today...

_____

_____

_____

_____

Thought to ponder as I sleep...

_____

_____

_____

_____

"Respond; don't react. Listen; don't talk. Think; don't assume."

Raji Lukkoor

I am grateful for...

_____

_____

_____

_____

My Mindful Moments today...

_____

_____

_____

_____

Thought to ponder as I sleep...

_____

_____

_____

_____

"The practice of mindfulness begins in the small, remote cave of your unconscious mind and blossoms with the sunlight of your conscious life, reaching far beyond the people and places you can see."

Earon Davis

I am grateful for...

_____

_____

_____

_____

My Mindful Moments today…

_____

_____

_____

_____

Thought to ponder as I sleep...

_____

_____

_____

_____

"Water, if you don't stir it, will become clear; the mind left unaltered will find its own natural peace."

Unknown

I am grateful for...

_____

_____

_____

_____

My Mindful Moments today...

_____

_____

_____

_____

Thought to ponder as I sleep...

_____

_____

_____

_____

"Be kind whenever possible. It is always possible."
Dalai Lama

I am grateful for...

My Mindful Moments today…

Thought to ponder as I sleep...

"Always hold fast to the present. Every situation, indeed every moment, is of infinite value, for it is the representative of a whole eternity."

Johann Wolfgang von Goethe

I am grateful for...

_____

_____

_____

_____

My Mindful Moments today...

_____

_____

_____

_____

Thought to ponder as I sleep...

_____

_____

_____

_____

"Suffering usually relates to wanting things to be different than they are."

Allan Lokos

I am grateful for...

_____

_____

_____

_____

My Mindful Moments today...

_____

_____

_____

_____

Thought to ponder as I sleep...

_____

_____

_____

_____

"In this moment, there is plenty of time. In this moment, you are precisely as you should be. In this moment, there is an infinite possibility."

Victoria Moran

I am grateful for...

_____

_____

_____

_____

My Mindful Moments today…

_____

_____

_____

_____

Thought to ponder as I sleep...

_____

_____

_____

_____

"If we learn to open our hearts, anyone, including the people who drive us crazy, can be our teacher."
Pema Chödrön

I am grateful for...

_____

_____

_____

_____

My Mindful Moments today…

_____

_____

_____

_____

Thought to ponder as I sleep...

_____

_____

_____

_____

"The moment one gives close attention to anything, even a blade of grass, it becomes a mysterious, awesome, indescribably magnificent world in itself."

Henry Miller

I am grateful for...

_____

_____

_____

_____

My Mindful Moments today…

_____

_____

_____

_____

Thought to ponder as I sleep...

_____

_____

_____

_____

"Begin at once to live, and count each separate day as a separate life."

Seneca

I am grateful for...

My Mindful Moments today…

Thought to ponder as I sleep...

"The basic root of happiness lies in our minds; outer circumstances are nothing more than adverse or favorable."

Matthieu Ricard

I am grateful for...

_____

_____

_____

_____

My Mindful Moments today...

_____

_____

_____

_____

Thought to ponder as I sleep...

_____

_____

_____

_____

"If you concentrate on finding whatever is good in every situation, you will discover that your life will suddenly be filled with gratitude, a feeling that nurtures the soul."

Rabbi Harold Kushner

I am grateful for...

My Mindful Moments today...

Thought to ponder as I sleep...

"Happiness is your nature. It is not wrong to desire it. What is wrong is seeking it outside when it is inside."

Ramana Maharshi

I am grateful for...

My Mindful Moments today...

Thought to ponder as I sleep...

"If you want others to be happy, practice compassion. If you want to be happy, practice compassion."

Dalai Lama

I am grateful for...

_____

_____

_____

_____

My Mindful Moments today...

_____

_____

_____

_____

Thought to ponder as I sleep...

_____

_____

_____

_____

"Each morning we are born again. What we do today is what matters most."

Buddha

I am grateful for...

_____

_____

_____

_____

My Mindful Moments today…

_____

_____

_____

_____

Thought to ponder as I sleep...

_____

_____

_____

_____

"Writing can be an incredible mindfulness practice."

Jon Kabat-Zinn

I am grateful for...

_____

_____

_____

_____

My Mindful Moments today...

_____

_____

_____

_____

Thought to ponder as I sleep...

_____

_____

_____

_____

"You practice mindfulness, on the one hand, to be calm and peaceful. On the other hand, as you practice mindfulness and live a life of peace, you inspire hope for a future of peace."

Thich Nhat Hanh

I am grateful for...

_____

_____

_____

_____

My Mindful Moments today...

_____

_____

_____

_____

Thought to ponder as I sleep...

_____

_____

_____

_____

"We are awakened to the profound realization that the true path to liberation is to let go of everything."

Jack Kornfield

I am grateful for...

My Mindful Moments today...

Thought to ponder as I sleep...

"The place to be happy is here. The time to be happy is now."

Robert G. Ingersoll

I am grateful for...

_____

_____

_____

_____

My Mindful Moments today…

_____

_____

_____

_____

Thought to ponder as I sleep...

_____

_____

_____

_____

"It takes a little bit of mindfulness and a little bit of attention to others to be a good listener, which helps cultivate emotional nurturing and engagement."

Deepak Chopra

I am grateful for...

_____

_____

_____

_____

My Mindful Moments today...

_____

_____

_____

_____

Thought to ponder as I sleep...

_____

_____

_____

_____

"When you realize nothing is lacking, the whole world belongs to you."

Lao Tzu

I am grateful for...

My Mindful Moments today…

Thought to ponder as I sleep...

"The best way to capture moments is to pay attention. This is how we cultivate mindfulness. Mindfulness means being awake. It means knowing what you are doing."

Jon Kabat-Zinn

I am grateful for...

My Mindful Moments today...

Thought to ponder as I sleep...

"Everything is created twice, first in the mind and then in reality."

Robin S. Sharma

I am grateful for...

_____

_____

_____

_____

My Mindful Moments today…

_____

_____

_____

_____

Thought to ponder as I sleep...

_____

_____

_____

_____

"Don't let a day go by without asking who you are... each time you let a new ingredient enter your awareness."

Deepak Chopra

I am grateful for...

_____

_____

_____

_____

My Mindful Moments today...

_____

_____

_____

_____

Thought to ponder as I sleep...

_____

_____

_____

_____

"Whatever the present moment contains, accept it as if you had chosen it. Always work with it, not against it."

Eckhart Tolle

I am grateful for...

_____

_____

_____

_____

My Mindful Moments today...

_____

_____

_____

_____

Thought to ponder as I sleep...

_____

_____

_____

_____

"We have only now, only this single eternal moment opening and unfolding before us, day and night."

Jack Kornfield

I am grateful for...

_____

_____

_____

_____

My Mindful Moments today...

_____

_____

_____

_____

Thought to ponder as I sleep...

_____

_____

_____

_____

"Mindfulness is about love and loving life. When you cultivate this love, it gives you clarity and compassion for life, and your actions happen in accordance with that."

Jon Kabat-Zinn

I am grateful for...

My Mindful Moments today...

Thought to ponder as I sleep...

"In the end, just three things matter: How well we have lived. How well we have loved. How well we have learned to let go."

Jack Kornfield

I am grateful for...

My Mindful Moments today...

Thought to ponder as I sleep...

"Observe the space between your thoughts, then observe the observer."

Hamilton Boudreaux

I am grateful for...

_____

_____

_____

_____

My Mindful Moments today...

_____

_____

_____

_____

Thought to ponder as I sleep...

_____

_____

_____

_____

"Mind is a flexible mirror; adjust it to see a better world."

Amit Ray

I am grateful for...

_____

_____

_____

_____

My Mindful Moments today...

_____

_____

_____

_____

Thought to ponder as I sleep...

_____

_____

_____

_____

"You have a treasure within you that is infinitely greater than anything the world can offer."

Eckhart Tolle

I am grateful for...

My Mindful Moments today…

Thought to ponder as I sleep...

"As soon as we wish to be happier, we are no longer happy."

Walter Landor

I am grateful for...

_____

_____

_____

_____

My Mindful Moments today…

_____

_____

_____

Thought to ponder as I sleep...

_____

_____

_____

_____

"Patience has all the time it needs."

Allan Lokos

I am grateful for...

My Mindful Moments today...

Thought to ponder as I sleep...

"Drink your tea slowly and reverently, as if it is the axis on which the earth revolves — slowly, evenly, without rushing toward the future; live the actual moment. Only this moment is life."

Thich Nhat Hanh

I am grateful for...

My Mindful Moments today…

Thought to ponder as I sleep...

"Mindfulness is the aware, balanced acceptance of the present experience. It isn't more complicated than that. It is opening to or receiving the present moment, pleasant or unpleasant, just as it is, without either clinging to it or rejecting it."

Sylvia Boorstein

I am grateful for...

_____

_____

_____

_____

My Mindful Moments today...

_____

_____

_____

_____

Thought to ponder as I sleep...

_____

_____

_____

_____

"You cannot control the results, only your actions."

Allan Lokos

I am grateful for...

My Mindful Moments today…

Thought to ponder as I sleep...

"In today's rush, we all think too much—seek too much—want too much—and forget about the joy of just being."

Eckhart Tolle

I am grateful for...

My Mindful Moments today...

Thought to ponder as I sleep...

"Feelings come and go like clouds in a windy sky. Conscious breathing is my anchor."

Thich Nhat Hanh

I am grateful for...

_____

_____

_____

_____

My Mindful Moments today...

_____

_____

_____

_____

Thought to ponder as I sleep...

_____

_____

_____

_____

"Mindfulness is simply being aware of what is happening right now without wishing it were different; enjoying the pleasant without holding on when it changes (which it will); being with the unpleasant without fearing it will always be this way (which it won't)."

James Baraz

I am grateful for...

_____

_____

_____

_____

My Mindful Moments today…

_____

_____

_____

_____

Thought to ponder as I sleep…

_____

_____

_____

_____

"It's only when we truly know and understand that we have a limited time on earth—and that we have no way of knowing when our time is up— that we will begin to live each day to the fullest, as if it was the only one we had."

Elisabeth Kübler-Ross

I am grateful for...

My Mindful Moments today...

Thought to ponder as I sleep...

"Today, like every other day, we wake up empty and frightened. Don't open the door to the study and begin reading. Take down a musical instrument."

Rumi

I am grateful for...

_____

_____

_____

_____

My Mindful Moments today...

_____

_____

_____

_____

Thought to ponder as I sleep...

_____

_____

_____

_____

"I wish that life should not be cheap, but sacred. I wish the days to be as centuries, loaded, fragrant."
Ralph Waldo Emerson

I am grateful for...

My Mindful Moments today…

Thought to ponder as I sleep...

"The way to live in the present is to remember that this, too, shall pass. When you experience joy, remembering that this, too, shall pass helps you savor the here and now. When you experience pain and sorrow, remembering that this, too, shall pass reminds you that grief, like joy, is only temporary."

Joey Green

I am grateful for...

_____

_____

_____

_____

My Mindful Moments today...

_____

_____

_____

_____

Thought to ponder as I sleep...

_____

_____

_____

_____

"There's only one reason why you're not experiencing bliss at this present moment, and it's because you're thinking or focusing on what you don't have…. But, right now, you have everything you need to be in bliss."

Anthony de Mello

I am grateful for...

_____

_____

_____

_____

My Mindful Moments today…

_____

_____

_____

_____

Thought to ponder as I sleep...

_____

_____

_____

_____

"Life is not lost by dying; life is lost minute by minute, day by dragging day, in all the small uncaring ways."

Stephen Vincent Benet

I am grateful for...

_____

_____

_____

_____

My Mindful Moments today…

_____

_____

_____

_____

Thought to ponder as I sleep...

_____

_____

_____

_____

"As long as we have practiced neither concentration nor mindfulness, the ego takes itself for granted and remains its usual normal size, as big as the people around one will allow."

Ayya Khema

I am grateful for...

My Mindful Moments today…

Thought to ponder as I sleep...

"Impermanence is a principle of harmony. When we don't struggle against it, we are in harmony with reality."

Pema Chödrön

I am grateful for...

_____

_____

_____

_____

My Mindful Moments today...

_____

_____

_____

_____

Thought to ponder as I sleep...

_____

_____

_____

_____

"The mind in its natural state can be compared to the sky, covered by layers of cloud which hide its true nature."

Kalu Rinpoche

I am grateful for...

My Mindful Moments today...

Thought to ponder as I sleep...

"If one were truly aware of the value of human life, to waste it blithely on distractions and the pursuit of vulgar ambitions would be the height of confusion."

Dilgo Khyentse Rinpoche

I am grateful for...

My Mindful Moments today…

Thought to ponder as I sleep...

"Knowledge does not mean mastering a great quantity of different information, but understanding the nature of mind. This knowledge can penetrate each one of our thoughts and illuminate each one of our perceptions."

Matthieu Ricard

I am grateful for...

_____

_____

_____

_____

My Mindful Moments today...

_____

_____

_____

_____

Thought to ponder as I sleep...

_____

_____

_____

_____

"The most precious gift we can offer others is our presence. When mindfulness embraces those we love, they will bloom like flowers."

Thich Nhat Hanh

I am grateful for...

_____

_____

_____

_____

My Mindful Moments today...

_____

_____

_____

_____

Thought to ponder as I sleep...

_____

_____

_____

_____

"To diminish the suffering of pain, we need to make a crucial distinction between the pain of pain, and the pain we create by our thoughts about the pain. Fear, anger, guilt, loneliness, and helplessness are all mental and emotional responses that can intensify pain."

Howard Cutler

I am grateful for...

My Mindful Moments today...

Thought to ponder as I sleep...

"Things falling apart is a kind of testing and also a kind of healing."

Pema Chödrön

I am grateful for...

_____

_____

_____

_____

My Mindful Moments today...

_____

_____

_____

_____

Thought to ponder as I sleep...

_____

_____

_____

_____

"Why, if we are as pragmatic as we claim, don't we begin to ask ourselves seriously: Where does our real future lie?"

Sogyal Rinpoche

I am grateful for...

_____

_____

_____

_____

My Mindful Moments today…

_____

_____

_____

_____

Thought to ponder as I sleep...

_____

_____

_____

_____

"Envy and jealousy stem from the fundamental inability to rejoice at someone else's happiness or success."

Matthieu Ricard

I am grateful for...

_____

_____

_____

_____

My Mindful Moments today...

_____

_____

_____

_____

Thought to ponder as I sleep...

_____

_____

_____

_____

"Mindful and creative, a child who has neither a past, nor examples to follow, nor value judgments, simply lives, speaks, and plays in freedom."

Arnaud Desjardins

I am grateful for...

_____

_____

_____

_____

My Mindful Moments today...

_____

_____

_____

_____

Thought to ponder as I sleep...

_____

_____

_____

_____

"The only thing that is ultimately real about your journey is the step that you are taking at this moment. That's all there ever is."

Eckhart Tolle

I am grateful for...

_____

_____

_____

_____

My Mindful Moments today…

_____

_____

_____

_____

Thought to ponder as I sleep...

_____

_____

_____

_____

"Our lives are lived in intense and anxious struggle, in a swirl of speed and aggression, in competing, grasping, possessing, and achieving, forever burdening ourselves with extraneous activities and preoccupations."

Sogyal Rinpoche

I am grateful for...

_____
_____
_____
_____

My Mindful Moments today...

_____
_____
_____
_____

Thought to ponder as I sleep...

_____
_____
_____
_____

"By breaking down our sense of self-importance, all we lose is a parasite that has long infected our minds. What we gain in return is freedom, openness of mind, spontaneity, simplicity, altruism: all qualities inherent in happiness."

Matthieu Ricard

I am grateful for...

_____

_____

_____

_____

My Mindful Moments today...

_____

_____

_____

_____

Thought to ponder as I sleep...

_____

_____

_____

_____

"Begin doing what you want to do now. We are not living in eternity. We have only this moment, sparkling like a star in our hand—and melting like a snowflake."

Francis Bacon Sr.

I am grateful for...

My Mindful Moments today…

Thought to ponder as I sleep...

"Life is a preparation for the future; and the best preparation for the future is to live as if there were none."

Albert Einstein

I am grateful for...

_____

_____

_____

_____

My Mindful Moments today...

_____

_____

_____

_____

Thought to ponder as I sleep...

_____

_____

_____

_____

"We spend precious hours fearing the inevitable. It would be wise to use that time adoring our families, cherishing our friends, and living our lives."

Maya Angelou

I am grateful for...

My Mindful Moments today...

Thought to ponder as I sleep...

"Why do they not teach you that time is a finger snap and an eye blink, and that you should not allow a moment to pass you by without taking joyous, ecstatic note of it, not wasting a single moment of its swift, breakneck circuit?"

Pat Conroy

I am grateful for...

_____

_____

_____

_____

My Mindful Moments today...

_____

_____

_____

_____

Thought to ponder as I sleep...

_____

_____

_____

_____

"Being mindful means that we suspend judgment for a time, set aside our immediate goals for the future, and take in the present moment as it is rather than as we would like it to be."

Mark Williams

I am grateful for...

My Mindful Moments today...

Thought to ponder as I sleep...

"Each step along the Buddha's path to happiness requires practicing mindfulness until it becomes part of your daily life."

Henepola Gunaratana

I am grateful for...

_____

_____

_____

_____

My Mindful Moments today...

_____

_____

_____

_____

Thought to ponder as I sleep...

_____

_____

_____

_____

"Walk as if you are kissing the Earth with your feet."

Thich Nhat Hanh

I am grateful for...

My Mindful Moments today…

Thought to ponder as I sleep...

"Every time we become aware of a thought, as opposed to being lost in a thought, we experience that opening of the mind."

Joseph Goldstein

I am grateful for...

_____

_____

_____

_____

My Mindful Moments today...

_____

_____

_____

_____

Thought to ponder as I sleep...

_____

_____

_____

_____

"Concentration is a cornerstone of mindfulness practice. Your mindfulness will only be as robust as the capacity of your mind to be calm and stable. Without calmness, the mirror of mindfulness will have an agitated and choppy surface and will not be able to reflect things with any accuracy."

Jon Kabat-Zinn

I am grateful for...

My Mindful Moments today...

Thought to ponder as I sleep...

"The greatest communication is usually how we are rather than what we say."

Joseph Goldstein

I am grateful for...

_____

_____

_____

_____

My Mindful Moments today…

_____

_____

_____

_____

Thought to ponder as I sleep...

_____

_____

_____

_____

"Meditation is essentially training our attention so that we can be more aware—not only of our own inner workings but also of what's happening around us in the here and now."

Sharon Salzberg

I am grateful for...

My Mindful Moments today...

Thought to ponder as I sleep...

"Wherever you are, be there totally."

Eckhart Tolle

I am grateful for...

_____

_____

_____

_____

My Mindful Moments today…

_____

_____

_____

_____

Thought to ponder as I sleep...

_____

_____

_____

_____

"The idea has come to me that what I want now to do is to saturate every atom. I mean to eliminate all waste, deadness, superfluity: to give the moment whole; whatever it includes. Say that the moment is a combination of thought, sensation, the voice of the sea. Waste, deadness, come from the inclusion of things that don't belong to the moment; this appalling narrative business of the realist, getting on from lunch to dinner; it is false, unreal, merely conventional."

Virginia Woolf

I am grateful for...

My Mindful Moments today...

Thought to ponder as I sleep...

"What you are looking for is what is looking."
Joseph Goldstein

I am grateful for...

_____

_____

_____

_____

My Mindful Moments today…

_____

_____

_____

_____

Thought to ponder as I sleep...

_____

_____

_____

_____

"If you miss the present moment, you miss your appointment with life. That is very serious!"

Thich Nhat Hanh

I am grateful for...

_____

_____

_____

_____

My Mindful Moments today...

_____

_____

_____

_____

Thought to ponder as I sleep...

_____

_____

_____

_____

"Meditate... do not delay, lest you later regret it."
Buddha

I am grateful for...

_____

_____

_____

_____

My Mindful Moments today...

_____

_____

_____

_____

Thought to ponder as I sleep...

_____

_____

_____

_____

"Flow with whatever may happen and let your mind be free: stay centered by accepting whatever you are doing. This is the ultimate."

Chuang

I am grateful for...

_____

_____

_____

_____

My Mindful Moments today…

_____

_____

_____

_____

Thought to ponder as I sleep...

_____

_____

_____

_____

"You can't stop the waves, but you can learn to surf."

Jon Kabat-Zinn

I am grateful for...

_____

_____

_____

_____

My Mindful Moments today…

_____

_____

_____

_____

Thought to ponder as I sleep...

_____

_____

_____

_____

"When you do something, you should burn yourself up completely, like a good bonfire, leaving no trace of yourself."

Shunryu Suzuki

I am grateful for...

_____

_____

_____

_____

My Mindful Moments today…

_____

_____

_____

_____

Thought to ponder as I sleep...

_____

_____

_____

_____

"Practice is this life, and realization is this life, and this life is revealed right here and now."
Maezumi Roshi

I am grateful for...

_____

_____

_____

_____

My Mindful Moments today…

_____

_____

_____

_____

Thought to ponder as I sleep...

_____

_____

_____

_____

"Emotion arises at the place where mind and body meet. It is the body's reaction to mind."

Eckhart Tolle

I am grateful for...

_____

_____

_____

_____

My Mindful Moments today...

_____

_____

_____

_____

Thought to ponder as I sleep...

_____

_____

_____

_____

"Use every distraction as an object of meditation and they cease to be distractions."

Mingyur Rinpoche

I am grateful for...

My Mindful Moments today…

Thought to ponder as I sleep...

"Now is the future that you promised yourself last year, last month, last week. Now is the only moment you'll ever really have. Mindfulness is about waking up to this."

Mark Williams

I am grateful for...

My Mindful Moments today…

Thought to ponder as I sleep...

"Wanting to reform the world without discovering one's true self is like trying to cover the world with leather to avoid the pain of walking on stones and thorns. It is much simpler to wear shoes."

Ramana Maharshi

I am grateful for...

_____

_____

_____

_____

My Mindful Moments today…

_____

_____

_____

_____

Thought to ponder as I sleep...

_____

_____

_____

_____

"As I noticed feelings and thoughts appear and disappear, it became increasingly clear that they were just coming and going on their own.... There was no sense of a self owning them."

Tara Brach

I am grateful for...

_____

_____

_____

_____

My Mindful Moments today...

_____

_____

_____

_____

Thought to ponder as I sleep...

_____

_____

_____

_____

"Meditation is the only intentional, systematic human activity which, at bottom, is about not trying to improve yourself or get anywhere else, but simply to realize where you already are."

Jon Kabat-Zinn

I am grateful for...

My Mindful Moments today...

Thought to ponder as I sleep...

"Your vision will become clear only when you look into your heart. Who looks outside, dreams. Who looks inside, awakens."

Carl Jung

I am grateful for...

My Mindful Moments today…

Thought to ponder as I sleep...

"Ardently do today what must be done. Who knows? Tomorrow, death comes."

Buddha

I am grateful for...

_____

_____

_____

_____

My Mindful Moments today…

_____

_____

_____

_____

Thought to ponder as I sleep...

_____

_____

_____

_____

"Let us spend one day as deliberately as Nature, and not be thrown off track by every nutshell and mosquito's wing that falls on the rails. Let us rise early and fast or break fast, gently and without perturbation; let company come and let company go, let the bells ring and the children cry—determine to make a day of it."

Henry David Thoreau

I am grateful for...

My Mindful Moments today…

Thought to ponder as I sleep...

"Awareness is the greatest agent for change."
Eckhart Tolle

I am grateful for...

_____

_____

_____

_____

My Mindful Moments today…

_____

_____

_____

_____

Thought to ponder as I sleep...

_____

_____

_____

_____

"Reality is only an agreement — today is always today."

Zen Proverb

I am grateful for...

My Mindful Moments today...

Thought to ponder as I sleep...

"Sit. Be still. And listen… for you are drunk and we are at the edge of the roof."

Rumi

I am grateful for...

_____

_____

_____

_____

My Mindful Moments today…

_____

_____

_____

_____

Thought to ponder as I sleep...

_____

_____

_____

_____

"The significance is hiding in the insignificant. Appreciate everything."

Eckhart Tolle

I am grateful for...

My Mindful Moments today…

Thought to ponder as I sleep...

"Throughout this life, you can never be certain of living long enough to take another breath."

Huang Po

I am grateful for...

_____

_____

_____

_____

My Mindful Moments today…

_____

_____

_____

_____

Thought to ponder as I sleep...

_____

_____

_____

_____

"If you live the sacred and despise the ordinary, you are still bobbing in the ocean of delusion."
Linji Yixuan

I am grateful for...

My Mindful Moments today…

Thought to ponder as I sleep...

"Guilt, regret, resentment, sadness, and all forms of nonforgiveness are caused by too much past and not enough presence."

Eckhart Tolle

I am grateful for...

_____

_____

_____

_____

My Mindful Moments today…

_____

_____

_____

_____

Thought to ponder as I sleep...

_____

_____

_____

_____

"Mindfulness, the Root of Happiness."
Joseph Goldstein

I am grateful for...

_____

_____

_____

_____

My Mindful Moments today…

_____

_____

_____

_____

Thought to ponder as I sleep...

_____

_____

_____

_____

"The real voyage of discovery consists not in seeking out new landscapes but in having new eyes."

Marcel Proust

I am grateful for...

_____

_____

_____

_____

My Mindful Moments today...

_____

_____

_____

_____

Thought to ponder as I sleep...

_____

_____

_____

_____

"I'm here to tell you that the path to peace is right there, when you want to get away."

Pema Chödrön

I am grateful for...

_____

_____

_____

_____

My Mindful Moments today...

_____

_____

_____

_____

Thought to ponder as I sleep...

_____

_____

_____

_____

"This is the real secret of life—to be completely engaged with what you are doing in the here and now. And instead of calling it work, realize it is play."

Alan Watts

I am grateful for...

My Mindful Moments today...

Thought to ponder as I sleep...

"The present moment is filled with joy and happiness. If you are attentive, you will see it."
Thich Nhat Hanh

I am grateful for...

_____

_____

_____

_____

My Mindful Moments today…

_____

_____

_____

Thought to ponder as I sleep...

_____

_____

_____

_____

"Pure awareness transcends thinking. It allows you to step outside the chattering negative self-talk and your reactive impulses and emotions. It allows you to look at the world once again with open eyes. And when you do so, a sense of wonder and quiet contentment begins to reappear in your life."

Mark Williams

I am grateful for...

My Mindful Moments today...

Thought to ponder as I sleep...

"Slow down and enjoy life. It's not only the scenery you miss by going too fast—you also miss the sense of where you are going and why."

Eddie Cantor

I am grateful for...

My Mindful Moments today...

Thought to ponder as I sleep...

"Today, you can decide to walk in freedom. You can choose to walk differently. You can walk as a free person, enjoying every step."

Thich Nhat Hanh

I am grateful for...

My Mindful Moments today…

Thought to ponder as I sleep...

*"Each morning we're born again
of yesterday nothing remains
what's left began today."*

Palladas

I am grateful for...

My Mindful Moments today...

Thought to ponder as I sleep...

"The art of living… is neither careless drifting on the one hand nor fearful clinging to the past on the other. It consists in being sensitive to each moment, in regarding it as utterly new and unique, in having the mind open and wholly receptive."

Alan Watts

I am grateful for...

_____

_____

_____

_____

My Mindful Moments today…

_____

_____

_____

_____

Thought to ponder as I sleep...

_____

_____

_____

_____

"What would it be like if I could accept life—accept this moment—exactly as it is?"

Tara Brach

I am grateful for...

My Mindful Moments today…

Thought to ponder as I sleep...

"What is it about our expectations, plans, or ideas that hold such sway over us? It is as if we've written a script for a play of our lives that runs about a month ahead of actual life; if reality varies from what we've created in our minds, we disengage or pout."

Holly Sprink

I am grateful for...

_____

_____

_____

_____

My Mindful Moments today…

_____

_____

_____

_____

Thought to ponder as I sleep...

_____

_____

_____

_____

"Mindfulness, also called wise attention, helps us see what we're adding to our experiences, not only during meditation sessions but also elsewhere."
Sharon Salzberg

I am grateful for...

My Mindful Moments today…

Thought to ponder as I sleep...

"The fundamental cause of grasping and rejecting, the source of all our pain, relies upon taking things—all our mental projections—as real."

Dzigar Kongtrul Rinpoche

I am grateful for...

_____

_____

_____

_____

My Mindful Moments today...

_____

_____

_____

_____

Thought to ponder as I sleep...

_____

_____

_____

_____

"It's not about approving or liking, but just being able to allow the world to be the way it is without resenting, hating, or judging it."

Buddhism Now

I am grateful for...

_____

_____

_____

_____

My Mindful Moments today...

_____

_____

_____

_____

Thought to ponder as I sleep...

_____

_____

_____

_____

"Human beings, by changing the inner attitudes of their minds, can change the outer aspects of their lives."

William James

I am grateful for...

_____

_____

_____

_____

My Mindful Moments today...

_____

_____

_____

_____

Thought to ponder as I sleep...

_____

_____

_____

_____

"My experience is that many things are not as bad as I thought they would be."

Mary Doria Russell

I am grateful for...

My Mindful Moments today…

Thought to ponder as I sleep...

"No one has ever been angry at another human being... we're only angry at our story of them."
Byron Katie

I am grateful for...

My Mindful Moments today...

Thought to ponder as I sleep...

"When you are present, you can allow the mind to be as it is without getting entangled in it."
Eckhart Tolle

I am grateful for...

My Mindful Moments today…

Thought to ponder as I sleep...

"We cannot be present and run our storyline at the same time."

Pema Chödrön

I am grateful for...

My Mindful Moments today…

Thought to ponder as I sleep...

"Every problem perceived to be 'out there' is really nothing more than a misperception within your own thinking."

Byron Katie

I am grateful for...

_____

_____

_____

_____

My Mindful Moments today...

_____

_____

_____

_____

Thought to ponder as I sleep...

_____

_____

_____

_____

"Few of us ever live in the present. We are forever anticipating what is to come or remembering what has gone."

Louis L'Amour

I am grateful for...

_____

_____

_____

_____

My Mindful Moments today…

_____

_____

_____

_____

Thought to ponder as I sleep...

_____

_____

_____

_____

"We withdraw from our experience of the present moment. We pull away from the raw feelings of fear and shame by incessantly telling ourselves stories about what is happening in our life."

Tara Brach

I am grateful for...

My Mindful Moments today...

Thought to ponder as I sleep...

"The standard way of reducing stress in our culture is to put as much energy as possible into trying to arrive at a moment that matches our preferences. This ensures that we feel some level of stress until we get there (assuming we ever will) and worse, it makes the present moment into an unacceptable place to be."

David Cain

I am grateful for...

My Mindful Moments today…

Thought to ponder as I sleep...

"We must be willing to encounter darkness and despair when they come up and face them, over and over again if need be, without running away or numbing ourselves in the thousands of ways we conjure up to avoid the unavoidable."

Jon Kabat-Zinn

I am grateful for...

My Mindful Moments today...

Thought to ponder as I sleep...

"We do so much, we run so quickly, the situation is difficult, and many people say, 'Don't just sit there, do something.' But doing more things may make the situation worse. So you should say, 'Don't just do something, sit there.' Sit there, stop, be yourself first, and begin from there."

Thich Nhat Hanh

I am grateful for...

_____

_____

_____

_____

My Mindful Moments today…

_____

_____

_____

_____

Thought to ponder as I sleep...

_____

_____

_____

_____

"If you aren't in the moment, you are either looking forward to uncertainty, or back to pain and regret."

Jim Carrey

I am grateful for...

My Mindful Moments today...

Thought to ponder as I sleep...

"Pain is not wrong. Reacting to pain as wrong initiates the trance of unworthiness. The moment we believe something is wrong, our world shrinks and we lose ourselves in the effort to combat the pain."

Tara Brach

I am grateful for...

My Mindful Moments today…

Thought to ponder as I sleep...

"The most fundamental aggression to ourselves, the most fundamental harm we can do to ourselves, is to remain ignorant by not having the courage and the respect to look at ourselves honestly and gently."

Pema Chödrön

I am grateful for...

My Mindful Moments today...

Thought to ponder as I sleep...

"All beings want to be happy, yet so very few know how. It is out of ignorance that any of us cause suffering, for ourselves or for others."

Sharon Salzberg

I am grateful for...

My Mindful Moments today...

Thought to ponder as I sleep...

"The energy of mindfulness has the element of friendship and loving kindness in it."

Thich Nhat Hanh

I am grateful for...

My Mindful Moments today…

Thought to ponder as I sleep...

"By learning to allow different types of discomfort to simply stay in the room with you, without your scrambling for a button to push (real or metaphorical), you make discomfort matter less. The pool of things you're afraid of shrinks. It becomes a lot less important to control circumstances, because you know you can handle moments of uncertainty or awkwardness or disappointment without an escape plan."

David Cain

I am grateful for...

_____

_____

_____

_____

My Mindful Moments today...

_____

_____

_____

_____

Thought to ponder as I sleep...

_____

_____

_____

_____

"Stepping out of the busyness, stopping our endless pursuit of getting somewhere else, is perhaps the most beautiful offering we can make to our spirit."

Tara Brach

I am grateful for...

_____

_____

_____

_____

My Mindful Moments today...

_____

_____

_____

_____

Thought to ponder as I sleep...

_____

_____

_____

_____

"Look at other people and ask yourself if you are really seeing them or just your thoughts about them."

Jon Kabat-Zinn

I am grateful for...

_____

_____

_____

_____

My Mindful Moments today…

_____

_____

_____

_____

Thought to ponder as I sleep...

_____

_____

_____

_____

"We often have very little empathy for our own thoughts and feelings and frequently try to suppress them by dismissing them as weaknesses."

Mark Williams

I am grateful for...

My Mindful Moments today...

Thought to ponder as I sleep...

"Essentially, meditation allows us to live in ways that are less automatic. This necessarily means less time spent worrying, ruminating, and trying to control things we can't control. It means we become less vulnerable to the throes of the fear-driven, older parts of our brains, and freer to use our newer and more sophisticated mental abilities: patience, compassion, acceptance, and reason."

David Cain

I am grateful for...

_____

_____

_____

_____

My Mindful Moments today…

_____

_____

_____

_____

Thought to ponder as I sleep...

_____

_____

_____

_____

"Acknowledging the pain and the suffering that take place inside you—and allowing the feelings—will take time, but this new way of handling these feelings will change the way you relate to you and to the outside world."

Kelly Martin

I am grateful for...

_____

_____

_____

_____

My Mindful Moments today...

_____

_____

_____

_____

Thought to ponder as I sleep...

_____

_____

_____

_____

"Somehow I always seem to forget the most powerful tool I have in my parenting arsenal: myself. My presence."

Carla Naumburg

I am grateful for...

My Mindful Moments today…

Thought to ponder as I sleep...

"Mindfulness has helped me succeed in almost every dimension of my life. By stopping regularly to look inward and become aware of my mental state, I stay connected to the source of my actions and thoughts and can guide them with considerably more intention."

Dustin Moskovitz

I am grateful for...

My Mindful Moments today…

Thought to ponder as I sleep...

"You might be tempted to avoid the messiness of daily living for the tranquility of stillness and peacefulness. This, of course, would be an attachment to stillness, and like any strong attachment, it leads to delusion. It arrests development and short-circuits the cultivation of wisdom."

Jon Kabat-Zinn

I am grateful for...

_____

_____

_____

_____

My Mindful Moments today…

_____

_____

_____

_____

Thought to ponder as I sleep...

_____

_____

_____

_____

"As we encounter new experiences with a mindful and wise attention, we discover that one of three things will happen to our new experience: it will go away, it will stay the same, or it will get more intense. Whatever happens does not really matter."

Jack Kornfield

I am grateful for...

My Mindful Moments today...

Thought to ponder as I sleep...

"Meditation is the ultimate mobile device; you can use it anywhere, anytime, unobtrusively."

Sharon Salzberg

I am grateful for...

_____

_____

_____

_____

My Mindful Moments today…

_____

_____

_____

_____

Thought to ponder as I sleep...

_____

_____

_____

_____

"True compassion is undirected and holds no conceptual focus. That kind of genuine, true compassion is only possible after realizing emptiness."

Tsoknyi Rinpoche

I am grateful for...

My Mindful Moments today…

Thought to ponder as I sleep...

"Mindfulness meditation should be more than just watching what you are doing. What you really need to watch is your motivation."

Lama Zopa Rinpoche

I am grateful for...

_____

_____

_____

_____

My Mindful Moments today...

_____

_____

_____

_____

Thought to ponder as I sleep...

_____

_____

_____

_____

"Mindfulness, as defined by the Buddha, means awareness of incessant change, of arising and vanishing, inside of your own body, which is the ultimate reality of your own life."

Paul Fleischman

I am grateful for...

My Mindful Moments today...

Thought to ponder as I sleep...

"We sit silently and watch the world around us. This has taken us a lifetime to learn... for silence is pure. Silence is holy. It draws people together... this is the great paradox."

Nicholas Sparks

I am grateful for...

_____

_____

_____

_____

My Mindful Moments today...

_____

_____

_____

_____

Thought to ponder as I sleep...

_____

_____

_____

_____

"When we are mindful of everything we are experiencing in the present moment, we separate our awareness from our thoughts."

Master Nomi

I am grateful for...

My Mindful Moments today…

Thought to ponder as I sleep...

"Mindfulness gives you time. Time gives you choices. Choices, skillfully made, lead to freedom. You don't have to be swept away by your feelings. You can respond with wisdom and kindness rather than habit and reactivity."

Bhante Henepola Gunaratana

I am grateful for...

_____

_____

_____

_____

My Mindful Moments today...

_____

_____

_____

_____

Thought to ponder as I sleep...

_____

_____

_____

_____

"Do not think that what your thoughts dwell upon is of no matter. Your thoughts are making you."

Bishop Steere

I am grateful for...

_____

_____

_____

_____

My Mindful Moments today…

_____

_____

_____

_____

Thought to ponder as I sleep...

_____

_____

_____

_____

"With mindfulness—the practice of peace—we can begin by working to transform the wars in ourselves. Conscious breathing helps us do this."
Thich Nhat Hanh

I am grateful for...

_____
_____
_____
_____

My Mindful Moments today...

_____
_____
_____
_____

Thought to ponder as I sleep...

_____
_____
_____
_____

"Life is denied by lack of attention, whether it be to cleaning windows or trying to write a masterpiece."

Nadia Boulanger

I am grateful for...

My Mindful Moments today…

Thought to ponder as I sleep...

"I think the one lesson I have learned is that there is no substitute for paying attention."

Diane Sawyer

I am grateful for...

_____

_____

_____

_____

My Mindful Moments today...

_____

_____

_____

_____

Thought to ponder as I sleep...

_____

_____

_____

_____

"Creativity, which is the expression of our originality, helps us stay mindful that what we bring to the world is completely original and cannot be compared."

Brene Brown

I am grateful for...

My Mindful Moments today...

Thought to ponder as I sleep...

"A man is literally what he thinks, his character being the complete sum of all his thoughts."

James Allen

I am grateful for...

My Mindful Moments today...

Thought to ponder as I sleep...

"It is better to travel well than to arrive."

Buddha

I am grateful for...

_____

_____

_____

_____

My Mindful Moments today...

_____

_____

_____

_____

Thought to ponder as I sleep...

_____

_____

_____

_____

"The capacity for delight is the gift of paying attention."

Julia Cameron

I am grateful for...

_____

_____

_____

_____

My Mindful Moments today…

_____

_____

_____

_____

Thought to ponder as I sleep...

_____

_____

_____

_____

"How much of your life do you spend looking forward to being somewhere else?"

Matthew Flickstein

I am grateful for...

My Mindful Moments today...

Thought to ponder as I sleep...

"Things which matter most must never be at the mercy of things which matter least."

Johann Wolfgang von Goethe

I am grateful for...

My Mindful Moments today…

Thought to ponder as I sleep...

"Restore your attention or bring it to a new level by dramatically slowing down whatever you're doing."

Sharon Salzberg

I am grateful for...

_____

_____

_____

_____

My Mindful Moments today...

_____

_____

_____

_____

Thought to ponder as I sleep...

_____

_____

_____

_____

"As long as we're caught up in always looking for certainty and happiness, rather than honoring the taste and smell and quality of exactly what is happening, as long as we're always running from discomfort, we're going to be caught in a cycle of unhappiness and discomfort, and we will feel weaker and weaker. This way of seeing helps us develop inner strength. And what's especially encouraging is the view that inner strength is available to us at just the moment when we think that we've hit the bottom, when things are at their worst."

Pema Chödrön

I am grateful for...

My Mindful Moments today…

Thought to ponder as I sleep...

"Luck is largely a matter of paying attention."
Susan M. Dodd

I am grateful for...

My Mindful Moments today…

Thought to ponder as I sleep...

"Sometimes the most important thing in a whole day is the rest we take between two deep breaths."
Etty Hillesum

I am grateful for...

My Mindful Moments today…

Thought to ponder as I sleep...

"The little things? The little moments? They aren't little."

Jon Kabat-Zinn

I am grateful for...

_____

_____

_____

_____

My Mindful Moments today…

_____

_____

_____

_____

Thought to ponder as I sleep...

_____

_____

_____

_____

"It's good to have an end in mind, but in the end what counts is how you travel."

Orna Ross

I am grateful for...

_____

_____

_____

_____

My Mindful Moments today…

_____

_____

_____

_____

Thought to ponder as I sleep...

_____

_____

_____

_____

"To be mindfully engaged is the most natural, creative state we can be in."

Ellen Langer

I am grateful for...

_____

_____

_____

_____

My Mindful Moments today…

_____

_____

_____

_____

Thought to ponder as I sleep...

_____

_____

_____

_____

"When I dance, I dance; when I sleep, I sleep; yes, and when I walk alone in a beautiful orchard, if my thoughts drift to far-off matters for some part of the time I lead them back again to the walk, the orchard, to the sweetness of this solitude, to myself."

Montaigne

I am grateful for...

My Mindful Moments today…

Thought to ponder as I sleep...

"Nature herself does not distinguish between what seed it receives. It grows whatever seed is planted; this is the way life works. Be mindful of the seeds you plant today, as they will become the crop you harvest."

Mary Morrissey

I am grateful for...

My Mindful Moments today…

Thought to ponder as I sleep...

"Instructions for life: Pay attention. Be astonished. Tell about it."

Mary Oliver

I am grateful for...

_____

_____

_____

_____

My Mindful Moments today...

_____

_____

_____

_____

Thought to ponder as I sleep...

_____

_____

_____

_____

"Mindfulness is the cure for everything; the essence of being alive."

Ellen Langer

I am grateful for...

_____

_____

_____

_____

My Mindful Moments today…

_____

_____

_____

_____

Thought to ponder as I sleep...

_____

_____

_____

_____

"Life is sweet when you pay attention. When it doesn't seem sweet, put a sticker on your nose and do a funky dance."

Whitney Scott

I am grateful for...

_____
_____
_____
_____

My Mindful Moments today…

_____
_____
_____
_____

Thought to ponder as I sleep...

_____
_____
_____
_____

Resources

Our Mindful Leader blog:
http://www.executivecoachinguniversity.com/blog

Our podcasts about all things mindfulness:
http://www.executivecoachinguniversity.com/blog/mindful-leader-podcast

Details on our Mindful Leader Workshop:
http://www.executivecoachinguniversity.com/landing/mindful_leader/

Our Mindful Movement page:
http://executivecoachinguniversity.com/mindfulness-movement#

Please visit:
www.ExecutiveCoachingUniversity.com/ to learn more about:
- Speaking and Facilitation
- Courses and Teleclasses
- Seminars and Workshops
- Coaching

Support@ExecutiveCoachingUniversity.com
or 1.800.251.1696

About A. Drayton Boylston

Greetings!

My name is Drayton Boylston. I feel privileged that you are reading this. Please know that I consider it such an honor that you would buy this book.

I write and teach about this amazing (and sometimes scary) adventure we are all on. I am simply here to help shed some light, provide some love, and offer up some tools that hopefully will help you along your path.

I am so very fortunate to be an internationally respected Coach, Author, Speaker, and now... Mindfulness Mentor. It is so cool that I can now use my background and experiences to serve others who are seeking a more peaceful life that provides inspiration and happiness.

While I had a crazy good ride in the corporate world as a former CEO and Fortune 100 executive, I am now blazing a much different trail through the second half of my life. This new trail of spiritual discovery has led me to shift my entire focus to help others along their own spiritual adventure. I see so much beauty in the gifts I have been given. My buttoned up corporate, "A," driver self now sees the "other side" of life. I now know exactly why I have been blessed with my unique journey.

I used to be one of those guys who didn't "get it" and, quite frankly, looked at folks who were doing mindfulness work as if they were from another planet. My personal mindfulness practice has helped me move beyond judgments like this. I know it can help you as well.

Just imagine... a big business guy becoming a Mindful Mentor?! I never would have guessed it 17 years ago. Now it is so cool to see how and why my journey has led me to this place. And while it may freak out some of my former colleagues, I know that all of us will eventually meet up in the same place....

Let's be clear up front... I don't have all the answers. What I do have is a sincere desire to help folks seek them. This doesn't have to be "out there" and "woo-woo" (it seems like it has been considered those things for waaay too long). I want to make this simple and approachable for everyone. I truly want to help bring mindfulness into the mainstream.™

I have had the privilege to teach thousands of beautiful souls in 39 countries... and counting.

My first book, *Coming UnScrooged!*™ *A Contemporary Classic of Corporate Rescue and Redemption* has garnered high praise from many quarters. With the addition of my two bestsellers, *A Whisper From Your Soul*™ and *More Whispers From Your Soul*™, I am blessed to have joined the ranks of highly respected authors as well. Just a couple of ways that I simply act as a conduit for important messages that I am here to share.

My forthcoming book *Woo-Woo Meets Wall Street*™ is sure to open some eyes.

With the launch of our International Mindfulness Federation in 2017, we are working hard to lead the charge to educate large numbers of people and organizations around the world on the benefits of leading a mindful life.

My sincere hope is that this book has reached you deeply and provided something that you needed.

Sending you peace, joy, and much love!

I may be reached at Support@ExecutiveCoachingUniversity.com or 1.800.251.1696.

For media and speaking inquiries, please visit: http://www.executivecoachinguniversity.com/learn-about-us/media-page